IDENTITY CRISIS

Where Do I Go From Here?

TRISTAN J. TOLBERT

WESTBOW
PRESS®
A DIVISION OF THOMAS NELSON
& ZONDERVAN

WestBow Press books may be ordered through booksellers or by contacting:

WestBow Press
A Division of Thomas Nelson & Zondervan
1663 Liberty Drive
Bloomington, IN 47403
www.westbowpress.com
844-714-3454

Because of the dynamic nature of the Internet, any web addresses or
links contained in this book may have changed since publication and
may no longer be valid. The views expressed in this work are solely those
of the author and do not necessarily reflect the views of the publisher,
and the publisher hereby disclaims any responsibility for them.

Any people depicted in stock imagery provided by Getty Images are models,
and such images are being used for illustrative purposes only.
Certain stock imagery © Getty Images.

All Scripture quotations are taken from the New King
James Version®. Copyright © 1982 by Thomas Nelson.
Used by permission. All rights reserved.

ISBN: 978-1-6642-0493-5 (sc)
ISBN: 978-1-6642-0492-8 (e)

Print information available on the last page.

WestBow Press rev. date: 09/30/2020

DEDICATION

This book is in dedication to anyone who has lost their way along this Christian Journey. There are times we hurt in silence. Sometimes we are shouting in the sanctuary but crying on our way home. It is my prayer that this collection of testimony be used to uplift, inspire, and motivate anyone with an Identity Crisis in Jesus name.

Contents

Call to Prayer ix

Introduction xi

1. Self-Worth 1
2. Healing 3
3. Truth Hurts 5
4. Love 6
5. Mental Health Part 1 8
6. Loving Others 10
7. Greatness Within You 12
8. Patience 14
9. Anxiety 16
10. Sleepless Nights 17
11. Trust Issues 19
12. Disappointment in Myself 21
13. Choosing your Circle 23
14. Choosing your Circle Part 2 25
15. Letter to My Younger Self 27
16. Leaving a Good Thing 29
17. Choosing Your Circle Part 3 31
18. The Dangers of Friendship 33
19. My Black is Beautiful 35

20. Significant Other 38

21. Are they the one? 40

22. Legacy 42

23. Letter to Myself #2 44

24. Mental Health Part 2 46

25. Disappointment in Others 48

26. So Hard to Say Goodbye 50

27. Agent of Change 52

28. Forgiveness 54

29. Until We Meet Again................................56

30. Where is Your Faith................................58

Letter to my Mentor 61

About the Author...63

Call to Prayer

Here I am, here I stand as a broken vessel to be used by your glory. I have made mistakes, I have been lost, I have been through valleys & and mountains but here I proclaim that you are God. You are my God. During my storms, you are my peace. Amid darkness, you are my light. In all that I do, I pray to be a living example of your Word. To become a beacon of light to show others to you. Let all those who may read of this covenant with thee, be blessed in the mighty and majestic name of Jesus. Amen.

Introduction

We have all encountered a place where life is between a rock and a hard place. Where it seems as if things go from bad to worse to incomprehensible. Our thoughts scatter to the point where we begin to question where God is in the midst of our troubles, circumstances, trials, tribulations, and distress is. If God is real, then why is all of this happening to me.

I have been in a place where I've asked God... "I've done this for you, and I've done that for you but why does this confuse me, frustrate me, and even cause me to lose my sanity?" But we have begun to ask the wrong question. I have learned that God does his best work in the middle of a troubled valley. It is in valley and the mountains, where God tests our very faith. If we only had good days, how would we know that God can turn our cloudy day's into sunshine? If we have never been sick, how could ever know that God can heal every disease? If we have never cried ourselves to sleep, how could we ever know that God can wipe all of our tears? If we never had our heart broken into pieces, how could we ever know that God is a heart fixer and a mind regulator?

God allows us to go through midnight to understand

that weeping may endure but for a night, but Joy will come in the morning. If you are going through a hard patch in life, my prayer for you is for you to reconnect with the one who is able to keep you, love you, sustain you, deliver you, hold you, and even care for you.

Father in the name of Jesus I come to you in the midst of a generation who has lost their connection to you. Father I pray that we go back to the old landmark and find that you were the same yesterday, today, and forever more. God, I pray that you continue to keep and watch over us we go through our various trials and tribulations and trusting you through the midst of it all. God remove anything and anyone who is deterring us from who you created us to be and begin to transform us into the creation we need to be to carry out your Word! It is in Jesus name I declare, Amen

Self-Worth

Having pride means that you hold yourself to higher standard and refuse to be belittled, degraded, and dethroned. Being born in your skin is not something you choose but something you begin to love about yourself. When God created you, he made you unlike any other. The Word says in Psalm 139:14, "I praise You, for I am fearfully and wonderfully made; Marvelous are Your works, and that my soul knows very well." Countless people cannot and sometimes are unwilling to understand you and wonder why you express yourself the way that you do. It is simply because they are not you. Some individuals even want to be you. The great thing is.... you know your worth. I know in your past you may have allowed people and places to use you, put you down, and cast you aside. That is the past. You cannot change that. What you can do is wake up every morning acknowledging that your time, your presence, your smile, your destiny, is worth more than anyone can ever imagine. Take time out today to understand that you are worth more than what you have allowed of others. God created you for a reason, a purpose, and a divine plan. Do not let the world tell you any different.

Father I thank you for memories of mistakes. You have allowed me to see something within me that could have never occurred if I were perfect. I am a work in progress. Continue to bless me with knowledge, understanding, and a willingness to keep pressing forward regardless of what life throws at me. In Jesus name….

Healing

Life has a way of placing us in situations where pain is unimaginable. Such circumstances will make you want to run away, cause depression, or even in worst cases consider suicide. Pain hurts even more when you have placed your entire heart and soul into a project, person, or thing. It seems as if you placed your full trust and reliance into something you cannot get your time, effort, or dignity back. There are even times when people are not even sorry about what happened or tell you that it is not as bad as it seems. "Everything is replaceable" they always say. Everyone deals with pain differently. We all move through life in a unique way. All I can say is.... the sun will shine again. Take your time. Move on your own timing! Do not allow the world to dictate what is in your heart. But you need to heal. Do not carry this pain to someone else to become hurt just like you. You deserve the time to find yourself again. When you find yourself, you will find your purpose. Just become the best version of yourself!

Father, I do not know what I am doing. I have lost my way and do not know where to go. Guide my mind, my footsteps, my words, my thoughts. Grant me encouragement to stay motivated while I am lost on my journey. Cover and keep me. In Jesus name

Truth Hurts

We live in a generation where the truth sounds like a knife cutting into us. Many of us honestly live in false realities and refuse to believe the reality of what is happening to us individually and collectively as a community. The truth of the matter is, to set our heart, mind, and spirit free, we must face the truth head on. We all have a different truth. May it be a decision we have to make, relationship gone toxic, or even people we must separate from. The truth will allow us to move past the hurt and the pain of yesterday by creating a view of what tomorrow could be. What is it that you are not willing to accept? How long have you been holding this in? How many nights have you cried about this? Wouldn't it just be better to let go and allow yourself to become free?

Father thank you for a spirit of honesty and search for truth. Guide me as I follow you as you enrich me with a season of release of pain, trials, and tribulation. Allow me to understand that the truth is meant to set me free from my bondage of living through lies, rumors, and stories. In Jesus name

Love

Love is not just an emotional but an action. Love will cause you to do crazy things from forgetting to place your personal needs first or chasing something that was never meant for your life. Love will also show you the path that you should go and allow yourself to find inner peace. Love also causes pain beyond reproach. But love can lead you to the person that is meant to be your help mate through this journey called life. Love is as love does but first you must love yourself. A preacher once said... how can you love someone you have never seen but cannot love the reflection in the mirror. Love means acceptance of who you are! From your downfalls, your mistakes, your tribulations, and your craziness. You cannot only love your good days; you must love the total package. The sad reality of it is... not all of us love ourselves. If I could push it, some of us hate the skin we live in. But you must first admit who you are. Secondly, understand you only have one life. Third, accept the life you are living. Fourth, and if you do not like your life... you are the only one who can change the direction you are in!

Father you are the true definition of love. Patient love. Kind love. Forgiving love. Understanding love. Teach me how to love like you. Change my thoughts to understanding/loving myself better so I can love someone else the way you see fit.

Mental Health Part 1

Many of us love to make sure others are ok before we even ensure our own mental health. We have abused ourselves by forgetting the major problems we have and in turn have drained us. Some of us suffer from depression, loneliness, a broken heart, or just overused. In a world where most people do not care about anyone but themselves, that places us in a terrible position. It is like placing you on a battlefield running into action as a medic but when you get there... there is a bomb planted just waiting for you. It hurts even more when you open your heart to people who do not even love themselves. Those people begin to take advantage of your kindness and leave you in the dust when they do not need you anymore. We must focus on ourselves more often. One person once asked.... I cannot help putting others first, how can I do that? By simply saying no sometimes. Schedule more things in the day for yourself such as reading time, more prayer, or even taking mental health trips. I never understood why the Grinch or Squidward did not like people much. After growing and being hurt several times, they just did not want to become hurt again. Something must have happened that caused them to lose trust in others. If that is, you.... take back your power. Go see a counselor/therapist. Pray more often. Say no more often. Love yourself.

Father guide my mind, my thoughts, my words, and my actions. Allow my head to be cleared and focused on thee. Change me oh God and allow me to become free. Allow my heart to be rebuilt and able to trust once again. For thy touch will make me whole.

Loving Others

We recently talked about loving yourself. How we have one life and that life is up to us to change! Also, how you cannot love anyone else until you love yourself. Loving others is key to your success in life. One of the church mothers always told me, "you may not like some people, but you have to love them in spite." Love will enable you to forgive those who have done you wrong. Grants you the ability to look past their mistakes/failures and see the best in them. Allows you to not become jealous or envious when they are blessed with something and it is not your time. Grants you the capacity to not treat people any kind of way. Strengthens you to help those in need such as homeless, children, and the elderly. Also provides the intelligence to RESPECT anyone regardless of sex, orientation, gender, class, status, and difference of opinion.

Can I tell you something? Loving others will EMPOWER you to become the best version of yourself. But since you are out here holding grudges, hating those in public elected offices, and despising those who hate the skin you live in; you will never become free to love yourself. You in turn give people power over you. Here is your word of the day.... LET THEM GO AND LOVE THEM! You do not have to like them to love them! Do not hold anything in your heart that will hurt your heart. Let go, be free, love everybody, and love the reflection in the mirror!

Father God in your Word you told us that love is a fruit of the Spirit! That when we love others the way they are supposed to be loved; we are loving you! So, Father renew in us a right spirit to love those not according to their works or deeds but by your divine love towards you us. For your Word says, "For All have sinned and fallen short of the glory of God." Romans 3:23.

Greatness Within You

You just do not understand yet how much greatness is within you! From your countless groundbreaking ideas to your unlimited potential.... but there is a problem. You do not believe it. Instead you believe the haters from family, friends, and even teachers. Let us call them your haters. The haters have adjusted your mindset to limit your creativity, growth, and potential. The haters have told you that you are just like another family member or just a thug or even you do not have the capacity to make it out of this classroom or even worse... that your ideas are impossible. Beloved, that's great news for you. Impossible is the beginning of greatness. Everything you see in the world was once an impossible idea. From the invention of the car to the light bulb, JEALOUS and ENVIOUS people have called those with brilliant ideas crazy beyond comprehension. I have peeked into your future and I see you opening your own business, becoming an author, and changing the entire world with your passion. Start talking yourself into stuff and not out of stuff. The last thing you need to do is convince yourself that you are amazing, and you deserve to try. You may not change the entire world the first time but keep trying! Change up your approach! One day... you will hit a breakthrough and the same haters that doubted you, will be right there asking how you accomplished such feat! You do not have to prove the haters wrong, just prove it to yourself.

Father you said in your Word that you know the plans for us, plans to prosper us and not harm us, to give us a future and a hope. Father I declare a new business, new ideas, new breakthroughs, and earned degrees over my life. That in all I do, it may glorify you. In Jesus name

Patience

Patience is a virtue. For generations we have said that some have it and some do not. But patience is an art that we all must master. It enables us to go through situations of life with ease and peace. It allows us to understand all vantage points of life. How can we continue in our destiny if we cannot be patient enough to work and pace ourselves to such point? I learned patience by being a church kid. My church was the definition of old school. Sunday school we sang hymns and was taught the ways of being responsible child of God. But the Sunday School review took forever and a day. Then when that was over... we have intermission of 15 min between Sunday school and morning service. During service it was more hymns, slow walking ushers, and a never-ending sermon. It taught me that we must endure to the end to finish the race. If I would have complained, it would have taken much longer. If I kept checking the time, time would go by slow minute by minute. But if I paid attention to my surrounding, participated in the service, and made friends along the way.... the journey will be worth the wait. Enjoy every moment you have. Do not rush anything. Time has a way of bringing the best things to us when we least expect it.

Father I thank you for a season of patience. It was during my waiting period that I found a quiet still voice to calm my spirit. Father instill in me a mind to wait on your promises, your will, and your way. That I might not rush my own will, but your will be done in my life. In Jesus name.

Anxiety

The definition of anxiety is distress or uneasiness of mind caused by fear of danger or misfortune. This has allowed us to cut things off too early, walk away from adventures & obligations prematurely, or give people the presumption that we will not follow through with what we promised. Anxiety will kill the destiny that has been planned over your life. We must move past our fear of history repeating itself and trying something that has never been done before. For you to move past it, you must move differently, gain knowledge, and pursue an offbeat way of thinking. If not, you will be trapped in a bubble of ordinary people, uniform mindset, and resembling pain. What is something that you have anxiety over? A new relationship? A new job? Meeting someone's family? A surgery? Or not becoming a statistic? You hold the power to your future and truth. Do not allow fear to dictate it. Like they say, "take the bull by the horns" and do something amazing with your life!

Father in your word, you declare, "do not be afraid" three hundred & sixty-five times. So, Father I declare it over my life each and every day and remember for you have not given me a spirit of fear but of POWER, LOVE, and a SOUND MIND! In Jesus name!

Sleepless Nights

O h, the dreaded nights where everyone is sound asleep, but you have a million thoughts running through your head. You have tried everything from hot tea to tiring yourself out, but nothing seems to help. Just you and your thoughts. From the mistakes you have made for the decisions you have to make to the people you care about.... Then out of nowhere comes the tears, the sadness, and the loneliness. What are we supposed to do in times like these? The old folks said you have your greatest ideas during sleepless nights or if they were churchy...maybe God is trying to tell you something. Today, focus on who you are in the now. Write down your thoughts raw in a journal. Note how you feel about those who are the closest to you. Record the things you want to say to them the most. Let them know how you feel. Spend time with those you have not reached out to in a while. Take a mental break and just relax. Do not run on empty. Be the person who can separate a bad day from a day of rest. Tell those around you that you love them. Hug someone harder/longer than ever before. Finally, let those tears fall. Refresh your life and see a major difference come tomorrow.

Father give us a spirit of rest. Rest in our thoughts. Rest in our spirit. Rest in our physical body. Save us from our thoughts and keep our mind stayed on thee. For you oh God are our refuge, a strong tower, a light in the darkness. For when we are weak, you are mighty, you are strong. Keep us when we cannot keep ourselves.

Trust Issues

Many of us suffer from a past of trusting the wrong person or institution. We have given much of ourselves to a person who did not have our best interests at heart. Such has led to denial, low self-esteem, heartache, depression, and even trust issues. In some cases, it has been a relative who overstepped their boundaries to a physical relationship to a boss who did not know your worth.... trust issues have forever changed who we are. The good thing about having trust issues is that we can recognize red flags quickly. Red flags such as, can only talk at a certain time of day/night, cannot tell anyone about the situation, lies are not adding up, or something is too good to be true.

Today, take power of your trust issues. First you must forgive whoever broke your trust. Secondly, release all ill feelings towards such person/institution. Next, turn your pain into love. This love will do three things. Love will enable you to trust others with caution, allow yourself to become mentally free from exhaustion, and the ability to educate someone else on past experiences of yours without bias. Finally, you must move on and trust yourself. Some of us are stuck in the past and in some cases, in the same very moment that hurt us. Let it go. Life is filled with swift transition. Do not let life pass you by.

Father I am grateful for my test. For it was in my test and tribulations that I found you to be a bridge over troubled water, a light in the darkness, a strong tower, my cornerstone.... Father in you I rely. I do not trust my instincts; I trust your Word. For in Word you declare that "Trust in the Lord with all of your heart and lean not unto thine own understanding. In all your ways acknowledge Him and He shall direct your path! I declare today I trust God with my thoughts, my actions, and my future. In Jesus name!

Disappointment in Myself

I found a letter that I wrote to my future self a long time ago. It was dated my freshman year of high school to my senior year of college. I had so many hopes, dreams, and goals that I had not even scratched the surface of. I laid the letter down and felt so disappointed in myself. How could I have done so much but so little all at the same time? It felt as if I have missed my own Golden ticket opportunity and have wasted my life until now. Such a moment placed me into a dark depressed state for a while. I ceased communication with people, deleted social media, and started to feel sorry for myself. This accomplished one thing.... it made me realize what I did not do. I know you are confused.

Let me help you. It helped me realize that life had other plans for me. Yes, I did not accomplish what I planned but that God had a different plan in mind. I touched so many lives, invested into a work that needed to be completed, and I had to find myself. Sometimes what you plan IS NOT your destiny. There are times when your plans must fall for the real divine plans for your life to propel into place. Do not waste time feeling sorry, look at what you have accomplished and be proud of yourself. Tell yourself everyday... "this may not be what I planned but it's better than what I could have imagined."

Father I thank you for a life planned before my existence. In your Word you declare to Jeremiah, "Before I formed you in your mother's womb, I knew you; Before you were born I sanctified you; I ordained you a prophet unto the nations." Father you have created us to do a great work to your people. Continue to cover and keep us as we press towards the mark, the high calling of Jesus Christ. In Jesus name.

Choosing your Circle

L ife is difficult in various ways such as schoolwork, becoming an entrepreneur, raising your credit score, and growing into the best version of yourself. There is a single denominator that always interrupts our thinking and delays the plans that we have set for our lives. It is simply our circle. Your circle is basically the people you talk to often that understand you. A group of friends/family that you trust enough over your wellbeing. The danger is when we place people close to us that are no good to our present and future. One person you cannot have in your circle is a hater. A hater cannot understand your dreams and goals because they are trying to downcast your future.

Secondly, a drama queen. A person that exaggerate everything in life to the point where it is impossible to become better with them around. Third is your frenemy/gossip. A frenemy is a person that portrays they are in your corner, but they are really telling your business in the street and alerting your real enemies of your plans. Lastly, a person with a negative mindset. A person with a negative mindset can't help but destroy your creativity, work, dreams, and aspirations by saying phrases like, "you can't", "you won't", "that's impossible", "you're not worthy", "your dreams are too big", "that's out of your budget and you'll never achieve it."

The crazy thing is you know these people and you keep them around because they are fun and always have a good time around them. These individuals are dangerous to your destiny. Here is what you do.... go to your friend list, contact list & follow list. Investigate every person on there and ask a simple question. If you cannot share your dreams and aspirations or get good advice from any one of them.... DELETE THEM! While we are at it, delete people who are stuck and do not want to move forward in life. We are cleaning house! It is time to surround yourself with people who not only believe in themselves but believe in you!

Father create in me discernment to choose wisely who is my enemy and who my destiny is connected with. Delete fake friendships in the name of Jesus. Discard those who are fun but cannot add to who I am in the name of Jesus. Surround me With those who are smarter than I am and who have a relationship with you in the mighty name of Jesus!

Choosing your Circle
Part 2

Life is simply an adventure. There are ups and downs, fire and ice, and people who question who you really are. Life questions the validity of the reason you get up every morning. It also questions why you continue with the same people every day. After deleting people out of my life, I found there are seven people who have showed me the path I needed to take to become a better version of myself.

First, it was the challenger. A challenger is someone that is smarter, more successful, and someone that is where you want to be. My challenger helped me realize that I did not know everything and pushed me past my comfort zone to a place of growth. Secondly, I needed a Convictor that believes in me and will not let me make unnecessary mistakes to mess with future I have destined for me. Someone that shows you their mistakes and worst moments to show you that you are not in this alone.

Next you need a counselor in your life. A counselor is someone who prays for you and that you can go to when life is going crazy. Someone that you can vent to and not be judged or worry your business will be in the street. A person that will give you advice may it be emotional, physical, or mental. The last we will discuss in this passage is a celebrator. A celebrator is someone that will not let you complain and be depressed. A person that presses you forward to enjoy life. Someone that reminds you what you have to offer the world and will not let you give up. That individual celebrates every small thing that occurs in your life so that you can have a flashback of what good has happened to you and tells you.... THE BEST IS YET TO COME!

Father thank you for placing certain individuals in my life that placed me in position to help someone else. To this day, I can still call on them and they will pray with me and for me. Father use me in a way that will glorify you in ways such as these for someone else. In Jesus name.

Letter to My Younger Self

Hey. I know everything is not perfect and there are some days where you want to give up. Just hang in there. Life is simply an adventure. We have had some crazy times and there will just get even wilder from here. But I must tell you a few things before I go. First, stop letting people get in your head. Their opinion does not matter. After high school, you will never see any of them again, especially your inner circle. Do what is best for you, not them. Oh, please do not let your mother scheme you into majoring in medicine. It is your life, not hers. Secondly, take more chances. Dude you have so many ideas to change the world. You legit just held a massive rally at a predominantly black high school, went to the school board demanding your principal back, and your peers staged a walk out of school over this man.

You are going to change the world but stop being afraid of your own shadow. Be blunt. Tell people how you really feel. Lastly, humble yourself. You are not always right and going to burn a lot of bridges just because they seem to read you like a book. Take the constructive criticism. Stay planted in one place. I know you are not in a comfortable place right now but hold on. People know who you are. Your name is always in their head. Let time lift you, not your absence. If only I knew then what I know now. But no matter, everything happens for a reason. Every person you encounter, every decision you make, and every world event, is going to build you into an amazing person. Do not stop being great because of bad people. Be the example for generations of knowing you are not perfect, but you are still holding on to a promise.

Father it is in you that I live, breathe, and have my being. Father you created a person who has been through turmoil, but I am still yet pressing forward. God do not let me give up, throw in the towel, or walk away. Allow my voice, my presence to continue until the day you call me home to be with you. Do not shield be from circumstances but strengthen me through them. Change my mind mindset from defeated to victorious in the mighty name of Jesus!

Leaving a Good Thing

Temptation is an instrument that derails every good thing we have in life. Such as relationships, school, work, family, friends, and even diets. It just takes one small glance, one short lived conversation to lead you in the direction that could change your life. Why do we enter temptation? We believe that the grass is greener on the other side. We forget to do a pros and cons list to analyze the situation. We just believe the lies/tricks of whomever is making us feel good now. But never lose something/someone you love for the POSSIBILITY of something you will like. I am not telling you to become stuck in life but rather understand when you break your loyalty, it is hard to become trusted again.

The best thing to do is shield yourself from small conversations. If you feel like you cannot handle it, block that person. If they do not go away, contact the person in charge or the person you are with. It is a team effort to stay loyal. At the end of the day, if temptation takes your mind from what/who you are with, the heart cannot be divided. Matthew 6:24 says, "No one can serve two masters; for either he will hate the one and love the other." What is it that is tempting you to deter your life? What attention have you been giving it? Is it worth messing up your life and turning it into a show? Would you be able to forgive yourself after?

Father thank you for a season of leaving people behind. Some people I have held onto longer because of what they could do for me but in the end, I still held onto the hurt and pain. Thank you for giving me strength to walk away and during tribulation thank you for your peace that surpasses all understanding.

Choosing Your Circle
Part 3

We previously discussed a few people you need in your life such as a challenger, convictor, counselor, and celebrator. These individuals will lead you on the path of physical, mental, and emotional success. Today we add a few more important people. The first one for today is one of a kind. They show you that you are not perfect and will be your rock in times of confusion and madness. This person you can show your imperfections, weakness, and your worries to without fear of judgement. A person like this is called your confidant. Without this person, you will bottle up your emotions and dreams and will not be any good to the world around you.

Secondly, you will need a Compassionate. This person is your emotional contact. A compassionate checks on you often and asks the simple question, "how are you mentally" or "are you mentally tired?" The Compassionate is willing to listen to you cry and vent but at the same time give you peace of mind. Lastly, you will need a conferee. A Conferee is a mentee you can mentor and pass down knowledge and wisdom to. Showing them your mistakes and giving advice often.

This person is normally someone who acts like you or is going behind you in life with a similar dream.

No matter how messed up we can be, the knowledge of our memories can save a lost and confused generation. Hopefully, you have these people in your life already but If not, do not go searching for these individuals. They will come to you naturally. You are not alone in this world. You just must be willing to open up and take your coat off. Not everyone is trying to be your enemy but be careful not to show everyone your true colors.

Father send people my way who are willing to build me into the person you created me to become. Allow me to lose connections of people who are my enemy. Change my heart to allow my trust issues to not get in the way of a blessing you have sent.

The Dangers of Friendship

s a kid, I found it difficult to make friends and in place I made enemies. Not by what I did, but by countless bullies. I did have a small crew of my own. We laughed, joked, & played games together. But when the going got tough, I was left all alone. I can recall my best friend in 6th grade. Once 7th grade hit, the girls came, and he was nowhere to be found. So, the question I want to raise is, what is the difference between a true friend and an associate. A true friend is loyal, trustworthy, and willing to be there for you. An associate is a person that you converse with every now and then but, they are just a bunch meaningless laugh between you and them.

As I have grown older that definition has expanded. It is important not to keep people close to you. People either steal your work, take advantage of you, or just leave you hanging. As of right now, I have just one friend. It is literally me. It may sound sad, but I find peace within that. There are people I hang with, but can I depend on them? If I need them, can I talk to them about the depthless of my heart? If I call them, will they show up? If I needed an escape, will they open their arms? The sad reality is most of our "friends" will not. So, before you call someone a friend, know what they are not willing to do for you in your time of need. Some people are just meaningless conversations to make life go by faster.

Father we thank you for showing us what a true friend is. The old folks would say "ain't no friend like Jesus." He is there for you when others are not. He is always on the main line waiting to hear you vent and cry. Most of all Jesus is there to heal, save, and deliver.

My Black is Beautiful

Being African American in 2020 is summed up in one phrase, "where do we go from here." From police brutality to a dictator running America to a failed school system to being treated by the color of our skin and not by the content of our character. How can we grow up in a society where you must tell brown and black children you have to be extra careful because you are born with two strikes against you? Do not let the world give you a third one. We live in a society that if a black and a white man both committed the same crime, the white man will get parole and the black man will get life in prison. Where do we go from here? We scream from the mountain tops that our black lives matter.

First, we take pride in ourselves and begin to love ourselves. Stop demeaning each other regardless of sexual orientation, class, education, and unfortunate circumstances. Secondly, we take our black dollar and use it in black business. Stop getting FOOLED when a business uses "Black Lives Matter" as a profit scheme. Third, we must educate ourselves! We must place ourselves in position where we know where we have been, can analyze our current circumstances, and produce a future where all God's creatures are educated and treated equally. Finally, brown and black individuals must not give up! We gave up shortly after Zimmerman was acquitted. We gave up when Trump was acquitted. We gave up when Sandra Bland did not receive adequate justice.

Now is the time to keep pressing, keep fighting, keep educating, keep protesting, keep marching. Letting our voice be heard until freedom rings from every courthouse in the land of the free. Letting our presence be felt until justice is served in the White House. Making sure America realizes that one day, black men and women, white men and women, LGBT, and all can sing the old hymn "Lift Every Voice & Sing." "Lift every voice and sing till earth and heaven sing. Ring with the harmonies of Liberty. High as the list'ng skies. Let it resound loud as the rolling sea. Sing a song full of the faith that the dark past has taught us. Sing a song full of the hope that the present has brought us. Facing the rising sun of our new day begun. Let us march on 'til victory is won."

Father create in me a heart for Justice just like Jesus. Jesus was not killed but crucified by a plot by the priests, the romans, the Jews, and even the pharisees. Jesus was an enemy of the state. He was not crucified for healing the sick and giving sight to the blind. Jesus was crucified because he rattled the society to be a fair and just church as God had commanded it to be. Create in me a desire to stir up change in my neighborhood, my church, my city, my state, my country, and my world. Let me not get comfortable with homeless being left abused or children not getting the necessary education that they deserved. But build in me a fire that will never go out. That I am not an American first, but a Christian with the desires of my Father stirring in me. I declare this in the mighty name of Jesus!

Significant Other

Life is great until your friends start to pair off and you are either left alone or third wheeling. Third wheeling is horrible. You watch people laugh and have an amazing time and yet you are just wanting to get out of the house. But many of us have a problem finding someone. Some might say our standards are too high. Other would say our standards are not high enough.

Well I have a few questions you should consider when you are interviewing a person. First, are they goal oriented? Do they have a plan for the next 2 years, 5 years, 10 years from now? Do they plan to start a business, go to the military, start a trade, or go to school? This tells us that they can be independent and are head strong. Secondly, what is their relationship with their family? Are they close to their parents? If not, what happened? This is not true in every situation but the way someone treats their parents is a good indication of how they will treat and respect you. Third, what was the key problem in their past relationship? This question is to see what exactly happened and what are they willing to do to keep the potential relationship safe and secure.

Many times, there is one single issue in a person when it comes to their ex's. Sometimes it is a personality glitch from communication issues to expressing in love through fighting to limited attention. The last question you must ask yourself. Does this person fit your future? Now when you are in the moment of lovey dovey, you do not see the problems or the errors. So, before you commit, do a list of pros and cons of this person. Analyze if they are truly good for you. Will they take care of you and your feelings? Will they always be there to support you and not become jealous? Will they never lay a hand against you? Are they willing to understand you? Once you answer these questions, you will find out if they are really for you.

Father I thank you for relationships that were dead from the beginning. God connect me with the one who is willing to stand the test of time to pray with me, worship with me, trust you with me, and be able to change the world with your Word with me. Block potential relationships that will hinder my relationship with you! And Father prepare me into the person who would be ready for the person you send my way. In Jesus name.

Are they the one?

S o, you have been dating someone for a while and you are considering asking the question of should you two be a thing. Well here are some questions you should consider before committing to a full relationship. First, do they offer you peace? When life is giving you a lot to handle, can they be your escape amid chaos? Are they willing to not focus on the problem but allowing you to become free from confusion, stress, and even depression? Secondly, are they willing to give you actual advice not just become your yes person? Many times, we date people because they support whatever we do but not give us realistic advice of how wrong we may be in a situation. You do not need a yes person, you need a partner who can talk you through plans, ideas, and dreams to find the best path. Which leads to the next question... can you reach your highest potential with them next to you? Are they a bump in the road or a guiding light to get where you are headed? Can you still concentrate on your own path and still be connected? (In a new relationship, you are still two individuals. You must make sure you have a life outside of them. If you make your life all about them when they leave; what would you do?)

Lastly, do they make time for you or must find time for you? Let me explain. If they must find time for you, you are not part of their story. You are simply an add on that can do slight damage to the world they live in. If they make time for you, they are making you a priority. Do not take this lightly. If a person is willing to change the way they live just so you can be comfortable, have enough attention, and help make you happier (happiness is an individual thing. You cannot be happy with someone. If you are not happy by yourself), you have found an amazing individual who is willing to go out of their way to see about your mental health, family issues, work issues, inner circle problems, and so much more. Make sure the person you get in a relationship can consistently maintain these traits. If not, let them go.

Father, in the Garden of Eden, you created Adam a helpmate out of his rib. God cancel every relationship that I may pursue who was not divinely connected to me before the beginning of time. Connect me with the person you created me to be with to honor your glory so I may go with your Word to be fruitful & multiply and raise God fearing children. In Jesus name.

Legacy

What do you want to be known for? What mark are you planning on leaving this world? What impact have you left on those placed in your life? Today, you should do a flashback. Look back at who has changed your life forever. May it had been a teacher, neighbor, boss, or coworker. Recall how they made you into the person you are today. Also remember the individuals who made a negative impact on you. They may have been an awful relationship, friend, or even family member. All of these individuals changed your life in some type of way. What have you done for someone else? Well it is hard to answer that question right. Sometimes we help unintentionally by being ourselves.

That is great and all, but I want to focus on the intentional helping. Going out of our way to make an impact on at least one person daily. Some of us are so conceited that we think the world is all about us and some people are just looking for a handout. But consider if you were having a bad day and one stranger made your day instantly better. That is why we were created. Small impacts daily will set us up for a larger impact later. I challenge you for the rest of this month, leave a POSITIVE impact on someone you do not know! Let us see how much of a blessing you are to this world.

Father you placed me on this world to change the world through my faith and being an example of Jesus. It is my prayer that I continue to make a positive intentional impact on the people that you have placed in my life. Not just the people I know but strangers like you said in your Word. "I was naked and you clothed Me; I was sick and you visited Me; I was in prison and you came to Me." Matthew 25:36 Allow me never to take advantage of the blessings you have given me. Father I know it should have been me. It could have been me. It would have been me, but God I thank you for your unmerited grace and mercy. God, I thank you for the life you have given me. I thank you for the times when I was so ungrateful but yet you till looked beyond my sins and still blessed me. Create in me a grateful heart so that when I wake up early in the morning, I have another reason to shout and say Thank You. In Jesus name.

Letter to Myself #2

There is going to be an older woman that is a teacher at school who will change your life forever. Her name is Ms. Richburg. Ms. Richburg teaches AP English. Before you get all upset, I know English is one of your worst subjects. Ms. Richburg is going to change the way you view the world through writing in just two short years. She is going to teach you poetry, the love of reading/understanding, and most importantly, how to release your emotions. There will be times in your life when things go from bad to worse and you will not know how to cope with your problems. People/places will hurt you that you could not imagine. Writing will allow you release all energy may it be positive, negative, or in between.

You will never guess but thanks to her, you are going to publish a book soon. When you leave high school, you will not think much about Ms. Richburg, but I would do anything to just hug her and tell her thank you for believing in me when I didn't think too much of myself. Since I cannot thank her, WE'RE going to be that same impact on someone else. When you attend college, you will take a course called Introduction to Education. They will give you an assignment entitled, "Why Do You Want to Become a Teacher?" You will not have to think long, one name comes to mind, Ms. Richburg.

Before I go, I reread what she wrote in my yearbook. She simply says," there will never be another Tristan." I gave her a reason to smile even though when she asked for volunteers I kind of hid behind people. See you in a few years my love.

Father I thank you for the impact of THE Ms. Richburg. From the moment I first saw her, I knew there was something that would happen between us. I thank you for her persistence even when I was too hardheaded to take a chance on myself. Father create me into a powerful, impactful educator that will motivate students of all backgrounds to look beyond what they are in the now and prepare them for what is about to be. Father I thank you for a life of a worth living. In Jesus name.

Mental Health Part 2

Tragedies come in life by surprise. We never know when you will get into a car wreck, lose a loved one, or even try to leave this world on your own. It is even worse when we attempt to deal with tragedies and pain by yourself. Who would have known little kids being bullied would commit suicide to escape the pain? Who would have guessed pastors who love to preach and teach God's Word would commit suicide? There are countless people around this world who have thought about leaving this world simply because the rest of us did not check on our friends, family, or coworkers. The strongest people in our lives need the most attention. They are not only being strong for you but strong for themselves.

Sometimes believing in Christ is not enough to prevent suicide. Sometimes praying is not enough. I used to think Christians that go to a mental health advisor relationship with God was not strong. But it is just the opposite. There was one Sunday my pastor left me in charge and I had to give a message to the congregation. That week I just had a car wreck and I honestly complained why did the wreck not kill me. Things in life were not right and the wreck was my breaking point. I was literally mad at God. I was so mad that the message from Sunday got even harder to complete.

Saturday morning things changed. God literally paused my entire life and said look at your arms. Look at your legs. Look in the mirror. You do not look like what you have been through, but you do need to go get help by talking to someone. God gave me the simple message... Isaiah 38:1-5. He sees your tears, he heard your cry, you are not alone. That is all we need to hear from someone else. The ability to be there for others. You do not have to be strong alone. You have an entire community behind you! If you need mental help, your county health services offer free counseling! You are not alone!

Father I thank you for the low moments of my life. In those times, I completely forgot who you were to me. I paid more attention to my pain than the cross. But I had to look at what you did in my life. You saved my life and yet I was not even appreciative of it. God Thank you for correcting my mind to be fixed on not what happened but who saved my life. In Jesus name

Disappointment
in Others

Have you ever believed in a person to the point of it pains you to look at them after they have disappointed you? Disappointment is a crucial part of life. It limits the ability of having everything go your way. It authors a different reality of second chances, countless mistakes you learn from, and frustration. Disappointment hurts even more when you have placed a lot of energy into a project. The countless, sleepless nights, research, and money spent is nonrefundable. Can I push it? Disappointments in people will have you questioning reality. It is important never to place any person on a pedestal because no one is perfect. When you place someone on a pedestal, it places them on the same level as God. Everything they say or do is just simply perfection. Some of the people we place on pedestals are music artist, politicians, and even our parents.

As a kid I idolized my pastor. There was nothing he could do or say that would make me love him any less. When I needed someone to talk or vent to, he would always be there. But then I moved to another state. The calls became scarce and before I knew it, the person I looked up to the most is basically gone. I felt devastated but after that incident I had to realize that people come and go. It is up to me at the end of the day to move forward and not keep looking back. That I cannot be disappointed in others for long and hold the pain. I must break lose and go on to the next day before I disappoint myself and regret wasting time.

Father Ecclesiastes 3:1,11 declares, "1 To everything there is a season for every purpose under heaven. 11 He has made everything beautiful in its time. Also, He has put eternity in their hearts, except that no one can find out the work that God does from beginning to end." God thank you for the various seasons in my life. It is alright to mourn when I lose someone, but it is in your name, I have the strength to go on another day. Help me press forward as I do what you have called me to do. In Jesus name.

So Hard to Say Goodbye

Death is hard to handle. Everyone grieves differently. May it be the death of a friendship, career, a project, or even a loved one. Some of the phrases we hear at funerals are... "why not me?", "how could this happen?", "God must not be real if he let this happen." As I stood before my sisters-in-law casket, I felt lifeless as if things were supposed to be different, they had to be different. But accepting death and then moving on takes strength, courage, and endurance. My brother instructed me to render the eulogy for my late sister-in-law.

I was a freshman in college and I always knew my brother was a strong individual. When the death occurred, life shifted. I did not know my sister in law amazing well, but she made my brother into a better person. When I started to prepare for the eulogy, God instructed me to go to Mark 4:35-38. The message was entitled, "The Storm is Only Temporary." As I mounted the pulpit and overlooked the congregation, my eyes immediately sought my brother in tears weeping with his children. I have never seen my brother cry but to see him break down, hurt me to my core. I still had to be strong and I simply closed my eyes so the tears could just fall.

As the service went on, I kept looking at my notes as if God would just help me. I kept thinking, "what could I say to my brother to help." As I mounted the podium, God immediately took over. My pain, my sorrow, my tears simply went away. One key phrase I said in the eulogy was, "when the storm comes, it will shake the entire house. Things will never be the same, but we have to be confident in the fact that the SUN will shine again because the SON is never going to leave us nor forsake us. When you feel like you are alone and It seems as Jesus is asleep, keep calling his name. Scream, yell, shout his name until peace comes. Because peace is on the way." Selah

Father I stretch my hands to thee. No other help I know. If thou withdraw myself from thee, oh where shall I go. Thank you, God, for standing up when I did not have the strength nor the courage to stand up or speak. God in 2 Corinthians 12:9 it declares, "And he said to me, 'My grace is sufficient for you, for My Strength is made perfect in weakness.' Therefore, most gladly I will rather boast in my infirmities, that the power of Christ may rest upon me." God continue to be with me as I run this Christian race. The road may not be easy but as long as you are with me, I can run on just little while longer. In Jesus name.

Agent of Change

As the days go by and this world is in chaos, what am I to do? From riots to protests to gender inequality to children in cages, what can I do to change the world? By becoming an agent of change. Many of us say we have no voice, no cause, no channel to express ourselves or even our vote does not count. The way we are speaking is if as we are already defeated and given up. But I refuse to believe that the world is rigged, and my voice does not matter.

From the Montgomery Bus Boycott, where thousands almost bankrupted the Montgomery City Bus System to fight inequality by carpooling and walking to work for over a year to the millions of Americans who voted for Barack Obama to become the 44th President of the United States.... if only we believed we can change the world still. The only reason America is a nation is because they wanted to become free of the tyranny of England. England sent those of lower class and those excommunicated to found America. When America got tired of heavy taxation, America declared its independence with the Boston Tea Party and the U.S. Declaration of Independence!

When we as group of people are tired of the status quo, it shifts the world. Do not give up on changing the world. You have more power within you than those who want to keep the world the same. We have been battered, abused, targeted, lied to, and forgotten about long enough. It is time to change the world if not for you, but for the one who cannot speak, the one with disabilities, or the one who is trying to find themselves. Find your voice. Find your cause. Find your way. Once you find it, grab it by the horns and ride it through. Change begins first with an idea and a plan. What is yours?

Father ignite a generation that will stand up for social injustice for your name sake. For when Christ was on the Earth, he stood against the law and spoke of grace. Father create in us a heart to change the world to resemble a free society of people proclaiming life, liberty, and the pursuit of happiness. In Jesus name.

Forgiveness

As we march towards a new beginning, some of us hold on to the mistakes of yesterday. The people that we have hurt, the hours we cannot get back, and the memories that still haunt us. Yesterday cannot be changed. It is your past. You can only change the next minutes, hours, days, and the rest of your future. One of the things I have learned is that some people will never forgive you, apologize to you, and some will never want to see you again. You have to forgive yourself. I recall the times at my second church. One place I never imagined pain to be.

As I grew in leadership, there were those who were jealous, envious, and would do anything to hurt my spirit. There was a time when I was preparing a message for youth church and I had to present it to the pastor to approve it. He literally tore my message to pieces verbally. Countless people left that room in tears over a period of time. I have always learned that church was a place of healing and love but in that very place, it was simply filled with pain and sorrow. Minister Adams called me a few days later and said, "He is just afraid of your potential. Do not let him run you out of this church.

Let God handle them, and you have to forgive them. It's not for them, it's for your peace of mind." I cannot change what happened to me, but I did have the power to press forward. It would be a lie if I told you I forgave him then. I had a sincere hatred for that individual for years until one day I had to simply let go.

When you do not forgive someone, you give them power over you. Whenever you are around them, your mood immediately changes. I refuse to give anyone power over me. I simply forgive but never forget because my future is independent of their opinions and is ultimately dependent on what I do from here on out.

Father give me the strength to forgive those who were placed in my life to give me a difficult time. For God I know you continuously forgive me for my mistakes and shortcomings. I recall a preacher say, "If you can't forgive someone, why should God forgive you?" God create in me a clean heart and renew in me a forgiving spirit. Let nothing stay in my heart that is not like you. Change my heart, my thoughts, and my actions to resemble Christ. In Jesus name.

Until We Meet Again

As I race to the finish of this novel, I cannot but help to think of my late pastor, The Reverend Rodney George. When I traveled to the University of Alabama at Birmingham to pursue a degree in medicine, he welcomed me in like his own son. I cannot tell you how many memories that little church of 24 people changed within me to become a better individual.

Pastor George's favorite motto was, "I love you and there is nothing you can do about it." He was a man full of love and grace. I never idolized him, but he was a temporary Father figure that God granted me. Many times, he would try to recruit me to become a member of Alpha Phi Alpha and I would always say, "I don't dance." He would always just chuckle.

Pastor George taught me that even when I would get tired, lonely, depressed, or want to give up, that there is always someone rooting for you and depending on you to keep pressing on. They may never say a word to you or even see them, but they are praying for you always. When I heard the news of his passing, I felt so numb. I never got to say thank you for all he did. Hug him one last time. I did not even tell him how much he meant to me.

Pastor George was more than a pastor, he was my guardian angel. It is crazy how we never let people know how much they mean to us while they are living. Sometimes they need to hear it to stay encouraged. So, to you Pastor George, I sincerely dedicate this novel to your memory. I pray you are still proud of me as you always were. Thank you for the memories. Thank you for the laughs. Thank you for being a person I needed. Until we meet again...

God I just thank you for the life of my pastor. As you know he meant the world to me as I grew in Christ. I pray that I can pass on the knowledge that he gave to me into someone else that his spirit may live on. That his memory may not go in vain. In Jesus name.

Where is Your Faith

O
ne of the hardest decisions in life is the decision to walk away or keep trying. It would be dishonest of me to say that I have not considered giving up. Giving up the pulpit, turning in my ordination papers, and walking away. Life have continuously placed in a position to ask the question why. Why has the church turned from a place of healing to a place of disrespect? Why do bad things happen to good people? Why does life feel so empty?

There have been times I would pray and not feel God's Spirit. Times when I cried out the name of Jesus and still felt so alone. Where is God when you need him the most. But through my countless nights in tears, I found God. I did not find him in a sanctuary nor a prayer closet. I found God in my testimony. One of the Deacons at Hall Street Baptist Church used to always tell me that my sermons felt so real because I would always use my personal testimonies. That he could feel Christ power through my overcoming.

I am not your average young minister. I do not get excited over preaching or teaching. I get excited when it is just me and God. When I can hear his still small voice, which calms my soul. A long time ago I found out I did not whoop in my sermons nor did I run to buy robes, but I found solace in knowing God for myself.

So today, I challenge you to find God for yourself. It is good to hear your pastor preach and teach but God's Spirit hits different when you have a personal connection with him. On November 5, 2004, at the historic Virginia Street Baptist Church, I accepted Christ into my life. November 7, 2004, I was water baptized in the name of the Father, the Son, and the Holy Ghost. But it was not until later Christ took over my life fully.

I am not perfect. I am not the world's greatest preacher. I cannot sing or dance. But I am simply a servant of the most High God. In him I live, I breathe, and have my being.

God, I thank you for this soul who is reading this novel. I pray that you encourage them to keep going, keep fighting, keep praying, keep reading your Word, and keep trusting in You. God cover and keep them in the midst of their pain and sorrow. Grant them your peace that goes beyond all understanding. Allow them to feel your touch. God grant them your Spirit so that they may never feel lonely again. As we grow towards learning more about ourselves, God grant us the ability to be healed, set free, and delivered in the name of Jesus.

Letter to my Mentor

From the days of being in the mayor's office to the moments you sat with me during Grandparents day in elementary school, your presence has stayed the same. My life has been in countless directions, but you, I have always relied on. When I feel down, I can call you and hear, "Tristan we're so proud of you." Even when I feel as if life could not get any worse, I can hear you say, "you know I and Cathy love you." You came into my life connected to my brother through the Big Brothers, Big Sisters program. I would always brag that I know the mayor and I have even been to your house. I recall the moments we went fishing, driving, and even memories with a Dalmatian named Jasmine. Every second with you I lived as if it would never end. Now as I have grown older, you are still and always will be my family. Throughout life, we meet temporary and lifetime connections. I thank God daily that you are healthy, safe, and have the ability to still change the world through your gentle heart. If I have never said thank you, let me say it now. Thank you for all you have done and keep doing in my life. The memories are not finished, and we have many more to make. Until I see you again, just remember this one thought. "Love can get you through anything." A wise old mayor once told me that.

About the Author

Tristan Tolbert was born and raised in Hopkinsville, Kentucky. He grew up running through the halls of the Historic Virginia Street Baptist Church under the leadership of Dr. M. O. Fort. Tristan later moved to Montgomery Alabama where he was licensed as a gospel minister at Hutchinson Missionary Baptist Church under the leadership of Dr. G.W.C. Richardson Jr. on June 17, 2012. After graduating from Robert E Lee High School, he moved to Birmingham, Alabama to attend the University of Alabama at Birmingham. While in Birmingham, he found his beloved college church, Lively Stone Missionary Baptist Church under the leadership of Rev. Rodney George. This is also where he was ordained into the gospel ministry on September 13, 2015. Today, Tristan is an associate minister at the New Home Missionary Baptist Church under the leadership of Rev. Lee B. Walker Jr. Tristan is also a student at Auburn University at Montgomery pursuing a Bachelor of Science in Secondary Education in Social Science/ Political Science. Lastly, Tristan is the youth Advisor for the Montgomery Antioch District Association where he oversees the Youth Council, Youth Banquet, Youth 5th Sunday Fellowship, and countless other Youth worship/ community opportunities.

Printed in the United States
By Bookmasters